IN THE LIMELIGHT

A COLLECTION OF
CHESTER'S EASIEST PIANO MUSIC

by
Carol Barratt

GW00602705

Published by

Chester Music
14-15 Berners Street, London W1T 3LJ, UK

Exclusive Distributors:

Music Sales Limited
Distribution Centre, Newmarket Road,
Bury St Edmunds, Suffolk IP33 3YB, UK

Music Sales Pty Limited
20 Resolution Drive,
Caringbah, NSW 2229, Australia

Order No. CH77605
ISBN 978-1-84938-872-6
This book © Copyright 2011 Chester Music,
part of the Music Sales Group.

Printed in the EU

Your Guarantee of Quality
As publishers, we strive to produce every book
to the highest commercial standards.
The music has been freshly engraved and the book has
been carefully designed to minimise awkward page turns
and to make playing from it a real pleasure.
Particular care has been given to specifying acid-free,
neutral-sized paper made from pulps which have not been
elemental chlorine bleached. This pulp is from farmed
sustainable forests and was produced with special regard
for the environment.
Throughout, the printing and binding have been planned
to ensure a sturdy, attractive publication which should
give years of enjoyment.
If your copy fails to meet our high standards,
please inform us and we will gladly replace it.

www.musicsales.com

CHESTER MUSIC
PART OF THE MUSIC SALES GROUP

INTRODUCTION

The huge variety of styles in this collection of pieces from the *Chester's Easiest Piano* series is a reflection of just how much young pianists are capable of even at this early stage. There are original pieces by me, arrangements of folk songs and the occasional blues–based piece.

At times the fingering used has been specifically selected to improve certain techniques, for example on page 33, bar 4 of the left hand. Throughout the book many other pianistic techniques can also be spotted. There are even three pieces with optional singing parts, as singing and playing at the same time is a useful skill to develop and also improves musicianship.

All the pieces have been chosen with performance in mind and so are ideal for concerts and festivals – though they are equally enjoyable in your lessons and at home. They are presented in order of difficulty, though may be performed in any order you like.

Carol Barratt

CONTENTS

ON THE WING

Watch out! The tune is in the left hand.

French-Canadian Folk Song
arr. Carol Barratt

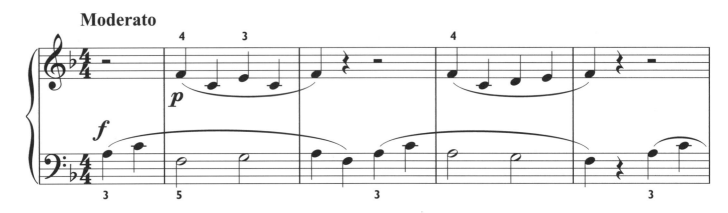

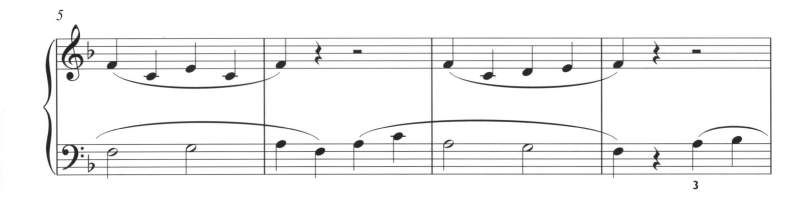

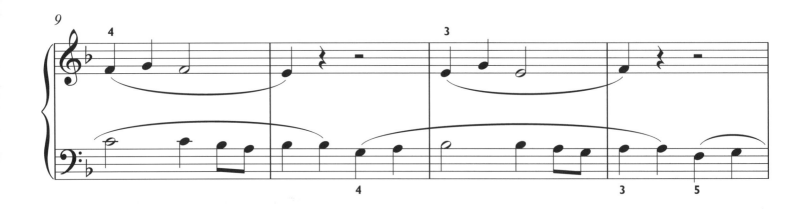

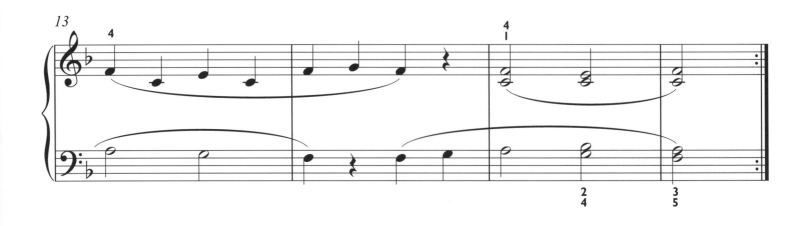

BLACK AND BLUES

Carol Barratt

Moderate blues tempo

Tap out the rhythms on the piano woodwork. (Optional)

[TO PLAY, OR PLAY AND SING]

PLANTING THE CABBAGE

(Savez-vous planter les choux?)

French Folk Song
arr. Carol Barratt

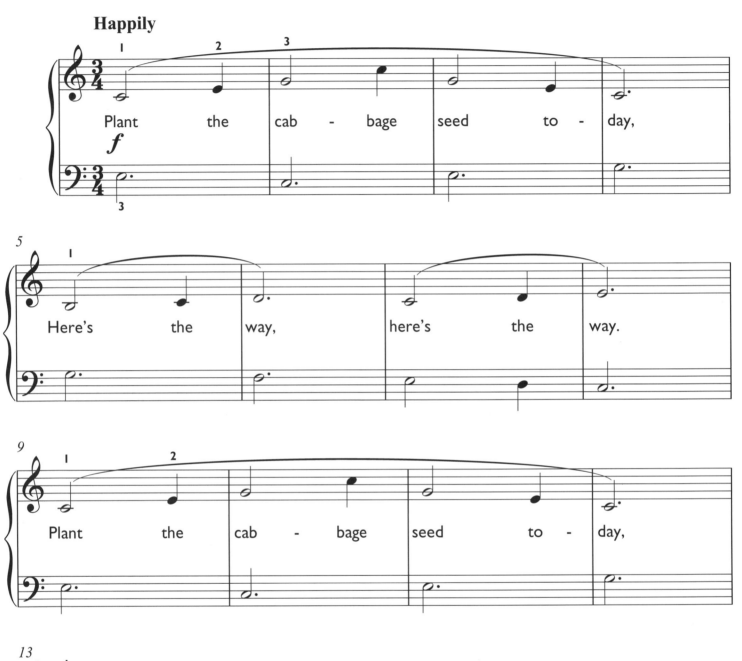

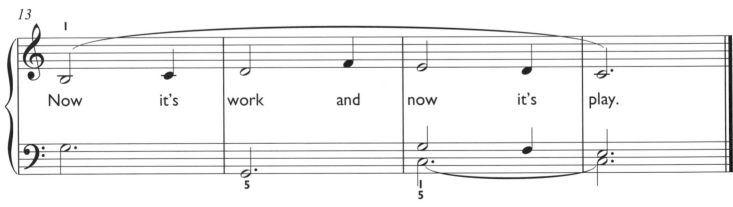

(Savez-vous planter les choux,
À la mode, à la mode?
Savez-vous planter les choux,
À la mode de chez nous?)

PROTOCERATOPS

Protoceratops is three metres long (about two bikes) and is a terrifying-looking, but friendly plant-eating dinosaur. It was the first horned dinosaur, though the horns were just bony lumps. It had a parrot-like beak and a 'frill' of bones on the skull.

Carol Barratt

WHOOPEE-TI-YI-YO!

American Cowboy Song
arr. Carol Barratt

Moderately slow

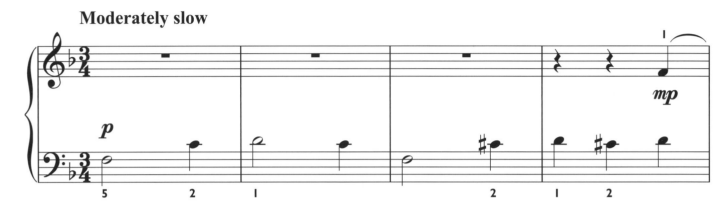

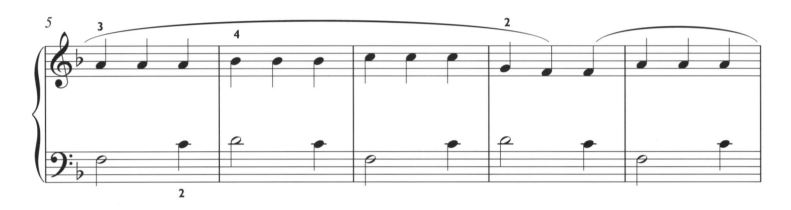

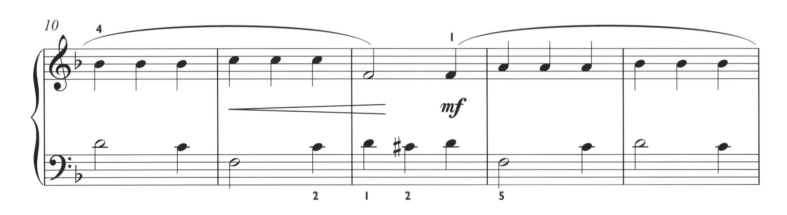

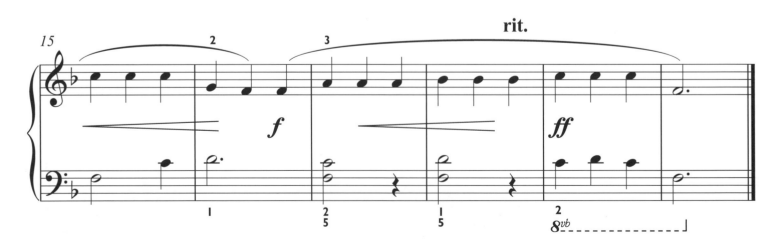

CLOWNS

Carol Barratt

DAVID OF THE WHITE ROCK

Welsh Folk Song
arr. Carol Barratt

TRICERATOPS

Triceratops was nine metres long (about two cars) and half of its length was its head.
The short nose horn and two brow horns jutting out from its head were used as
weapons. It was mean-tempered and powerful. Watch out!

Carol Barratt

With menace

Try adding the sustaining pedal to bars 9–16, either changing the pedal every bar or every two bars
for a special effect.

TARA'S RAG

Carol Barratt

DAME, GET UP AND BAKE YOUR PIES

Traditional
arr. Carol Barratt

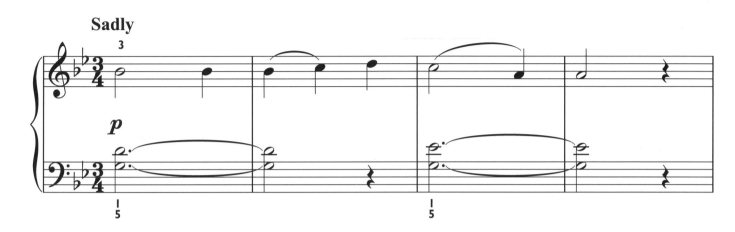

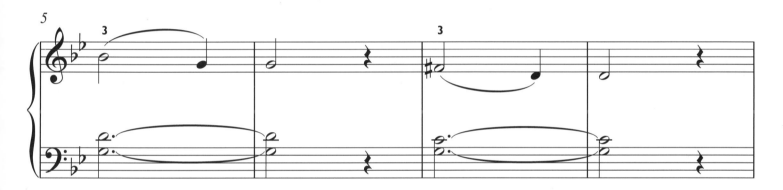

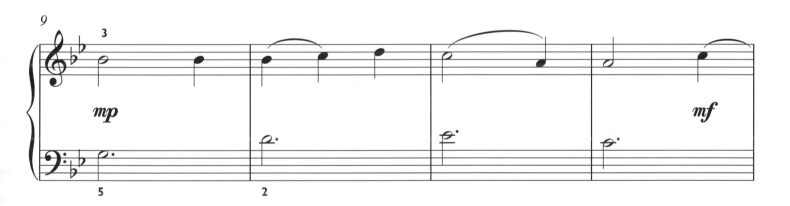

CHESTER WINS AGAIN!

Carol Barratt

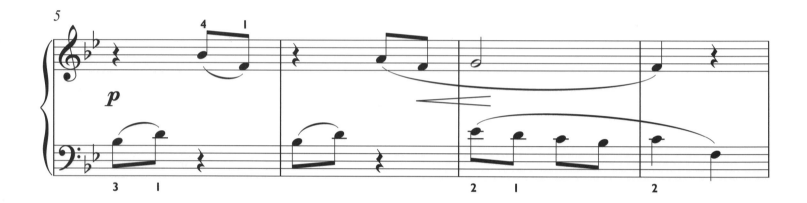

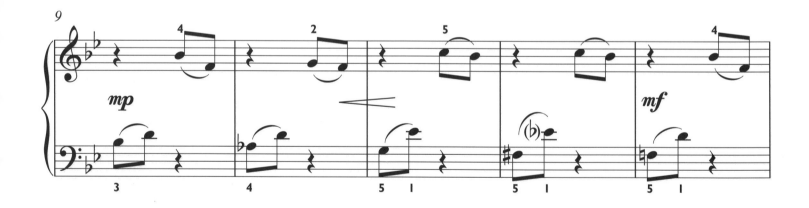

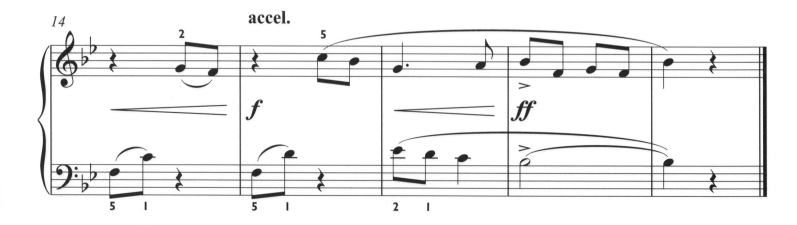

IGUANODON

Iguanodon was nine metres long (about two cars) and probably walked on all fours. It was a large, heavy plant-eater but had fearsome spiked thumbs for jabbing into enemies' eyes.

Carol Barratt

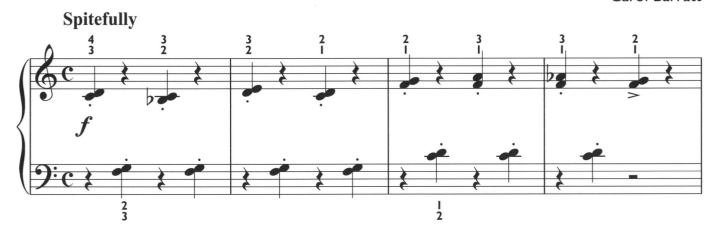

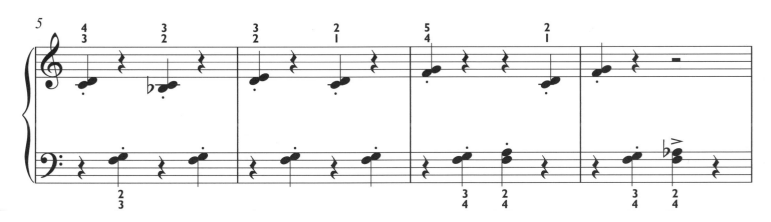

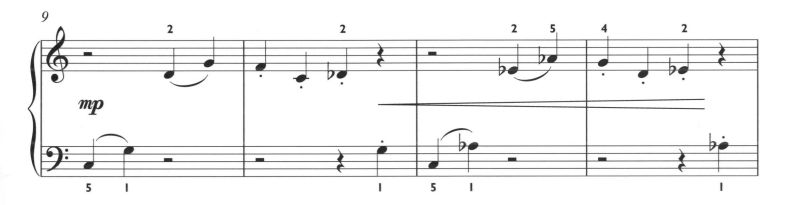

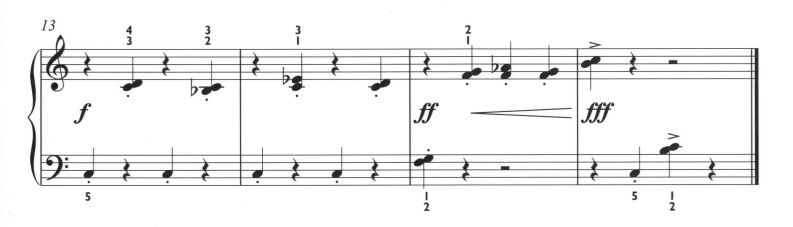

BARBARA ALLEN

English Folk Song
arr. Carol Barratt

[TO PLAY, OR PLAY AND SING]

BUBBLE AND SQUEAK

Carol Barratt

Greedily

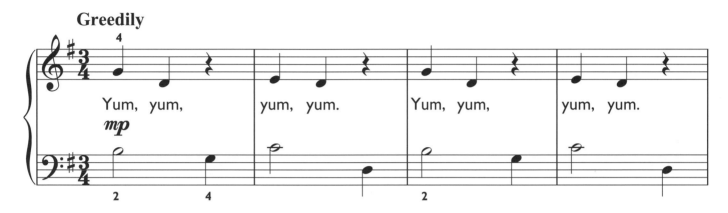

Yum, yum, yum, yum. Yum, yum, yum, yum.

mp

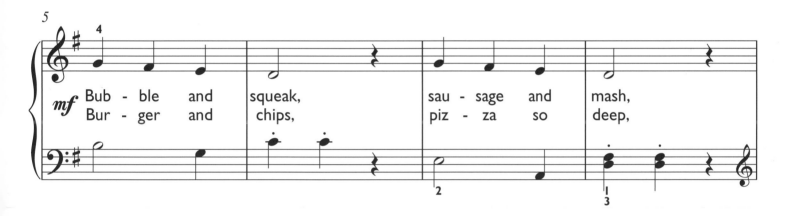

mf Bub - ble and squeak, sau - sage and mash,
Bur - ger and chips, piz - za so deep,

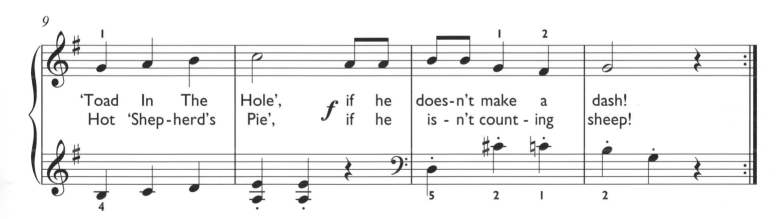

'Toad In The Hole', *f* if he does-n't make a dash!
Hot 'Shep-herd's Pie', if he is - n't count - ing sheep!

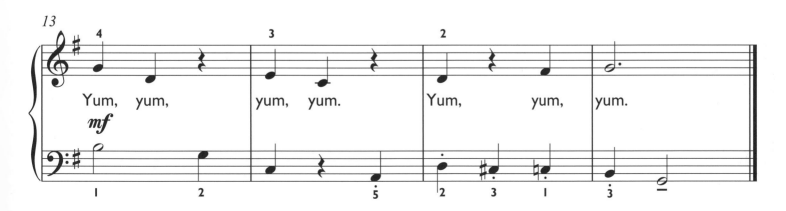

Yum, yum, yum, yum. Yum, yum, yum.

mf

OVER THE HILLS AND FAR AWAY

Traditional
arr. Carol Barratt

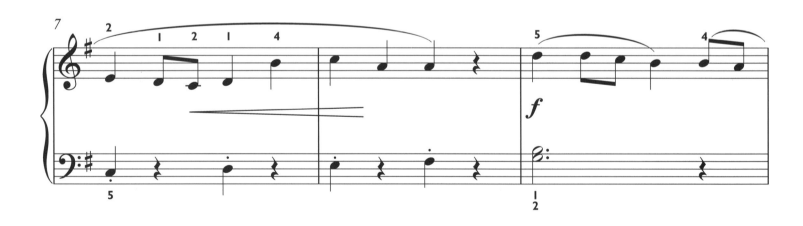

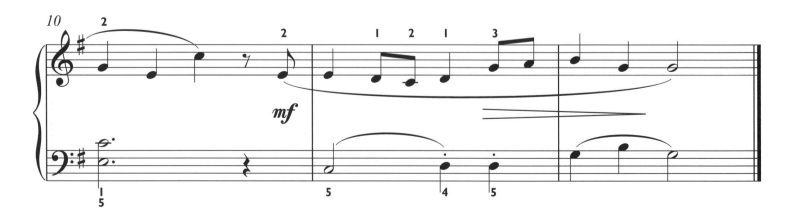

THE CAT IN THE CORNER

Irish Fiddle Tune
arr. Carol Barratt

TYRANNOSAURUS REX
Second Player

Tyrannosaurus Rex was fifteen metres long (about four cars) and five times taller than a man. It had bone-crushing jaws and knife-like teeth. It had a large head but tiny front legs and was a fast runner – despite its size!

Carol Barratt

COMPSOGNATHUS
First Player

*Compsognathus was about one metre long (two skateboards) with most of
its length in its tail. Its back legs were twice the length of its front legs and
it was a fast runner. It hunted lizards and insects in the forests.*

Carol Barratt

March tempo

WHEN I WAS A TAILOR

English Folk Song
arr. Carol Barratt

Busily!

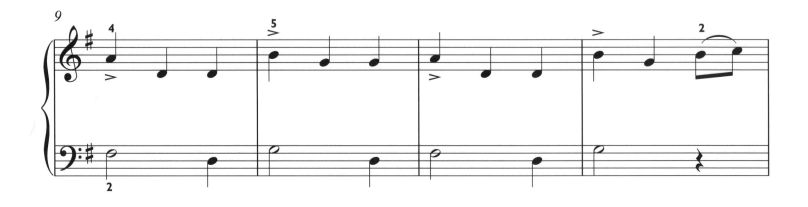

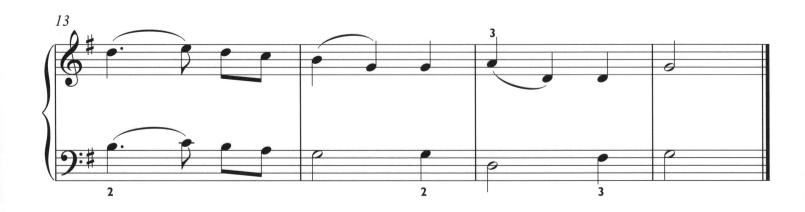

ALEXANDER MARCH

No one can be quite sure if Ludwig van Beethoven (1770–1827) or Carl Czerny (1791–1857) wrote this piece. Czerny was a pupil of Beethoven's and possibly heard him playing it!

Adapted from the composer (whoever he was!)
arr. Carol Barratt

THE JUNIPER TREE

American Folk Song
arr. Carol Barratt

NAOMI'S NUMBER

Carol Barratt

With a steady beat

[TO PLAY, OR PLAY AND SING]

MANNERS

Words: anon
Music: Carol Barratt

Cleverly

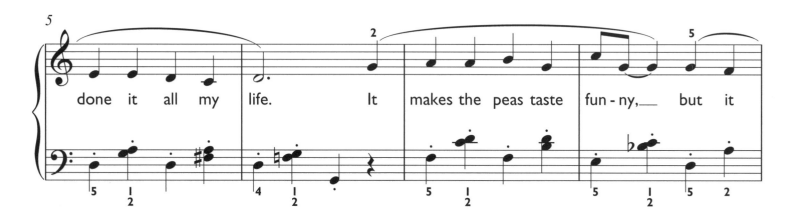

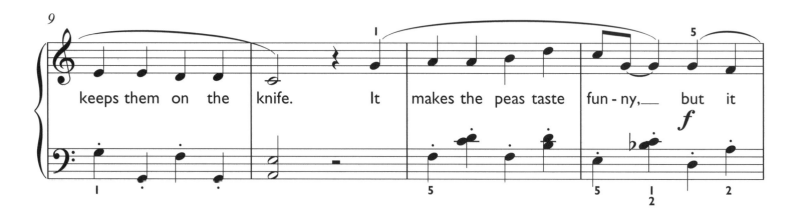

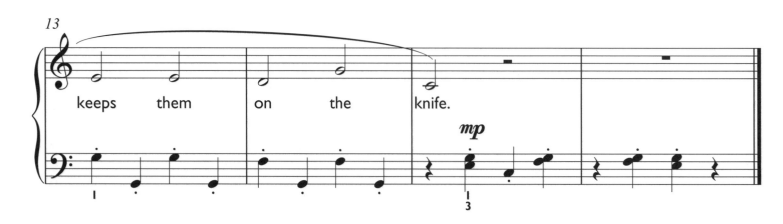

AUNTY LIZZIE'S OLD PIG

Carol Barratt

BRACHIOSAURUS

*Brachiosaurus was twenty-four metres long (about two large buses) and was the
heaviest animal ever weighing 85–110 tons (equal to fourteen elephants!). Its head
was about fourteen metres high, with two holes above the eyes. This plant-eater was
very slow and liked to stay in the water as it was easier to move!*

Carol Barratt

Slowly and heavily

TO MARKET, TO MARKET

English Folk Song
arr. Carol Barratt

With a lilt

SUPERFROG

Carol Barratt

THE CROW

This tune uses the pentatonic scale (five-note scale) which starting on C is:

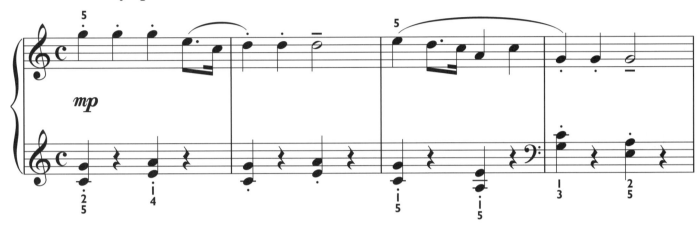

Chinese Folk Tune
arr. Carol Barratt

Leisurely speed

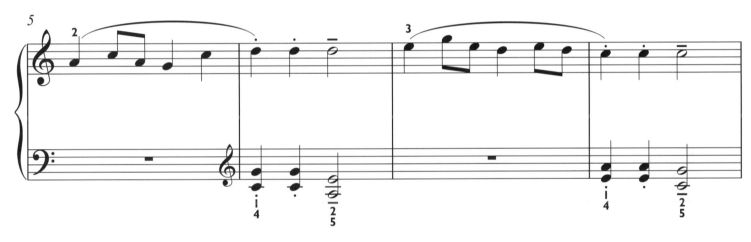

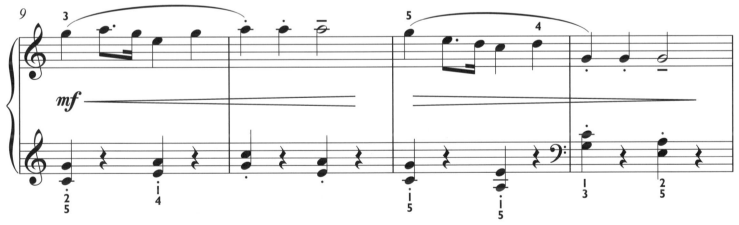

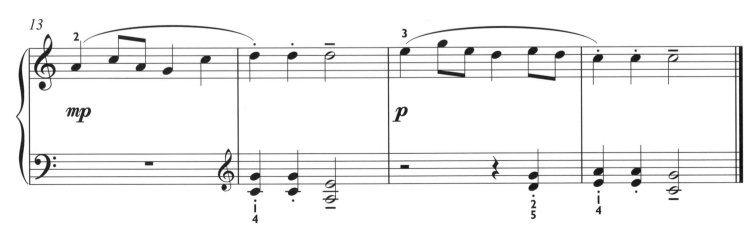

RAISINS AND ALMONDS

Jewish Folk Lullaby
arr. Carol Barratt

Slowly and gently

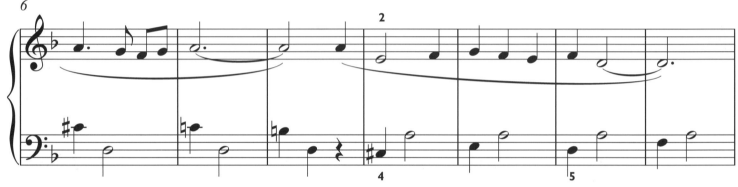

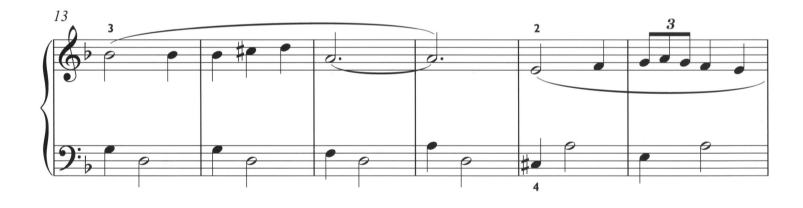

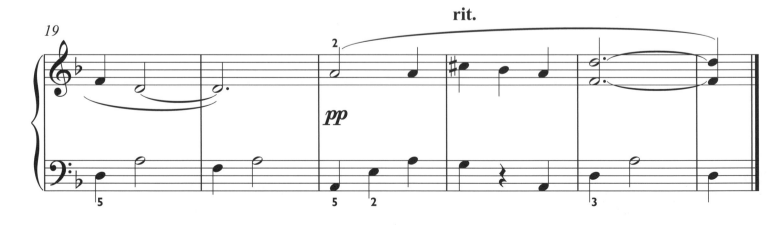

MARCH FOR A BLUE MONDAY

Carol Barratt

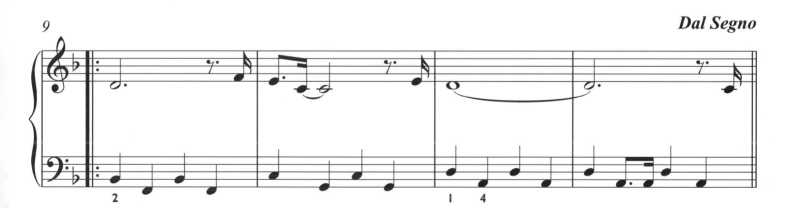

Bar 4 – tricky left-hand fingering

THE FOX JUMPED OVER THE PARSON'S GATE

English Folk Song
arr. Carol Barratt

DIPLODOCUS

*Diplodocus was twenty-six metres long (about seven cars) and had a
long, snake-like neck and tail. It had tree-trunk legs, a tiny head and
very small teeth. This gentle giant ate leaves high on the trees.*

Carol Barratt

With quiet contentment – stretching comfortably

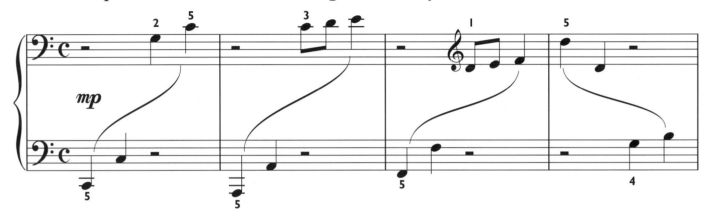

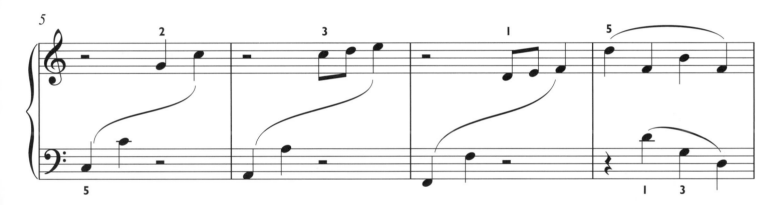

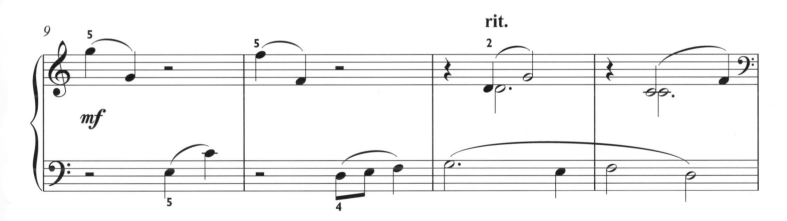

Try adding the pedal to this piece – change it every bar.

GIRAFFES

Carol Barratt

EARLY ONE MORNING

English Folk Song
arr. Carol Barratt

STROLLING SAM

Carol Barratt

OUT-OF-STEP MARCH

Watch out for the changing time signatures
which give this march its special character.

Carol Barratt

123456789

Chester's Easy-Peasy Theory Sets

Chester's Easy-Peasy Theory Sets 1, 2 & 3
give young children a real sense of enjoyment as
they begin to learn the language of music. The
worksheets are carefully graded to take into account
the development of pupil's reading and writing skills.
They can be used alongside any instrumental lessons or
methods and are suitable for young beginners aged 5
years and upwards

Theory Set 1	Order No CH73513
Theory Set 2	Order No CH73843
Theory Set 3	Order No CH77154

Taking You All The Way To Grade 1

UNDER & OVER
CHESTER'S EASIEST SCALE BOOK

...easy!

Under & Over is the easiest and best way to learn
to play scales properly! Taking the player from the
basics, it introduces scales progressively and works
through fun exercises (finger twisters!) to create solid
technique and musicianship for playing smooth,
steady and even scales. This foundation will make
an obvious difference to all performance pieces

The book contains everything you need to prepare for
both the Associated Board and Trinity Guildhall Grade 1
and Prep Test exams.

Order No CH75933

Written by Carol Barratt